Dedication

To My Truest Friend, Ryan Georgia,
May his Strength Last As Long As The Ink In This Book.

To All Of My Other Friends,
For Their Continuous Support And Inspiration.

To My Sister, Tori
For All Of Her Love, Advice, And Laughter.

And To The Memories Of Daniel
And Don Abernathy, And Jack Bradley;
With Hopes That They Are Happy And At Peace.

All day it fell slow snow
and I saw that
I am an independent being, devoid
of all
that I know.

When the heat vent comes on
in this room, the wooden floor
creaks and cracks, sounding
like the last dripping drops
of a rain storm ending
or a sputtering log on fire.
It is hot and cold both
under this uncovering blanket
of lifeless night — where
outside a streetlamp shimmers
a windshook tree through
the window shade.

I am formed in sleep,
unable to sleep.
But perhaps my dream
would only tell
me something I already know I feel;
maybe someday I'll show
like the rising sun
and emerge from this bone bath.

THOUGHTS, PERCEPTIONS,

and other

MISCELLANEOUS ABSTRACTIONS

by

Daniel J. Lutz

FIRST EDITION

UNIVERSITY EDITIONS, Inc.
1905 Madison Avenue
Huntington, West Virginia 25704

Cover photograph by tye jereme kirk
Cover design by Kimberly Raines

I am the music of the city:
screeching, piano banging, buses,
sirens, horns blaring blast,
a brick building being demolished,
another being built,

Subways, highways, lighters being flicked
in the bars, drunks in the street,
rainwater draining into sewers,
change jangled in cups held by the homeless,
whispers in the theater.

I am children at play
in the park after dark
and the dull din warning
of windchimes on the front porch
in the morning.

Table of Contents

Everything is a noise:
eyelids blinking are clock ticks,
the walls sigh in strain,
footsteps on the ceiling fall
and the forgetful nature of time
seems not so negative.
The red, wet highway drafts
through the unstripped
sliding glass door.
The cold drafts along also.
The dog lost behind the fence
looks for home; he sniffs
upon his paths of curiosity.
The autumn is wintry
and he leaves paws in old snow.
The sky, tiled in clouds
is filled with the moon,
while fields of street
grow untended.

Read These Words

Read my words
and laugh at your soul.
Read my words
dig holes beneath them
so that you may get underneath them.
Read my words
because it is for you
that I am plagiarizing ideas
from poems that I have yet to write.
Read my words
and realize
that there a worlds within
this world;
your world,
my world,
our world,
there is no world at all.
Read my words
and eat them like pearls,
they are for you only;
They are for me only.
They are for all of you only.
Read my words
and keep from being lonely.
Read my words
to formulate your own thoughts.
Read my words
let them invade you,
and become you;
steal a piece of me,
I am letting you
by letting you read my words.
Read my words
and know that
no matter how much I tell you,

you will still know nothing
about me
or my words.
Read my words.
Read my words
and fall farther
than you have ever fallen.
Read my words
and I will remove the ground
from below you.
Read my words
before they desecrate you.
Read my words
and become aware
of your own knowledge.
Read my words
and learn me.
Read my words
then burn me.
Read my words
I am reading you.
Read my words.

A Reason for Poetry

Poetry for the sake of poetry
Non-poetry for the sake of non-poetical poetry
Non-rhyming, no reason poetry
for the sake of justification of reality.
Reason for reality's sake
Sake for the sake of sakeness.
Poetry for the sake of
green, orange, pink, blue,
love, hate, emotion, art, non-emotion, non-emotional emotion,
correctness, monarcy, laughter, wrong, pain,
confusion, frustration.
Poetry for reasons of repression.
Depression.
Poetry to digress.
Poetry to elucidate.
Poetry for a little illiterate child
living in a far off, far away, fareast,
third world, no world country
sleeping in a bed of mud, under a hollow tree reed house.
Poetry about a desk,
for the sake of a floor about a chair.
Sleep, wake, dance, sing, live, die, DEATH,
breath, the absence of sanity, war, Indo China!
Poetry to stop breath, to cease life, to live in death.

Look out behind you!
Realign yourself.
Project yourself.
deject your-non-self.

Poetry about Autumn, fall,
leaves falling from Autumn's grace,
Winter, summer, heat, birth, myth,
glued brain powder.

Amidst the complete death and destruction of society,
social society, or non-social-non-societal society's Hiroshima:
the devastation of many hundreds of thousands of millions
of meaningless and intentional deaths;
Amidst the crumpled concrete and burnt steel;
Amidst the chaos of the end of the world;
Amidst all this, Poetry is a single, solitary purple Iris
growing out of the dank aftermath.

Clouds bury trees underwater and
Poetry is there.

When tree tops collapse coffins,
Poetry is the mastermind.
Love and emotion mantain the magic of Poetry,
but these do not transverse symbolic symbolism.

Lady Light loves lying lonely amoung
crystalically crisp and cracklingly clad clouds.

If Poetry was a black bird,
it would never leave its perch, nor would its song ever cease.
Poetry is a power higher and stronger than that of Nature.
Poetry is all things:
it is time,
a place,
a thought,
many thoughts,
it is a conversation that engages and detaches,
removes, and transports to a new realm of consciousness,
it is space; both outer and inner.
Poetry is just words on a piece of paper
Paper that never ends, never gives up, never gives in.
Poetry is poetry.

Upon Finding a Dead Bird in My Backyard

I had always heard the trees twittering,
but only thought of the songs
as a wonderful noise,
instead of as a creature;
a life living in my backyard; eating, sleeping, and traveling
throughout my backyard.

And after pondering the bird's death,
I arrived at the conclusion that:
poetry is the beauty
that comes from misery.

Stand Near

I have found myself
standing near
once hidden pastures of grain. Here,
the wind drowns time infinitely.
Your star, my present
from the world,
has created light
where once lived only dark.
Your heart
you may have given without your own assent,
but until now I have only
dreamed of your beauty.
The joy upon my visage
has destroyed the
dementia, anguish, and dread
that had burned within my
soul.
My destiny
was created the moment that
you walked in my sleep.

Her

She is my little love child;
she shows
    her
love like blue spilt wax
on a blue spilt rug.
She has
dancing skulls dancing about
    her
dancing feet and
magic mushrooms
growing from the floor in the
3-D light of
    her
3-D room.
She will nurse
    her
fattening 3-D baby while draping
    her
flaming 3-D mane about
    her
child's smoking face,
while telling stories of death
through triangulated contextualized art.
She keeps
    me
as
    her
last man at home
to make sure
that it is more than
my
death that is killing
me,
for my heart is mortal.
I

live in
    her
devil days, consuming
my
own stories of love struck demons,
frozen in their own subconscious.
She has
    her
avalanche of antelope
and is, therefore,
everything that
I
need, situated within
everything that
I
do not want; this
briskly sweeps
my
chairs away with dire efficiency, and
I
am left to track
    her
elusive Christmas trees and
    her
biting shelves, before they bite
someone else.
She makes
    me
aware that the meaning is in
the sound and that
I
should keep
    my
buckets filled with God and stock
    my
sealed jars of confidence
before the hibernation of

my
soul takes dominion
in the bleakness of
    her
candy lies.
She inspires
    her
ghouls, goblins, and ghosts
to revolt and force
    her
to be
free from
    her
dehabilitating culture of
metaphysical horses.
She has
    her
snake eye,
she has
    her
eagle eye,
she has
    her
spider dance
with a fly,
she has
    her
cricket minding its own business,
she has
    her
maggot of intention
curious about life,
she has
    her
mole with its hidden past,
she has
    her
pseudo-scorpion with its murderous mandibles,

13

she has
    her
aardvark destroying termite's skyscrapers, and
she has
    her
dead man sleeping in
my
bed, gently caressing
my
back with his rigor mortis fingers and
    her
structured silence.
She asks me to remember
all the times that she lost
    her
dimes and she has
    her
fourteen parts of fourteen equivocal sonnets
with a high ratio of low availability.
She has
    her
elephantine ballerinas dancing
their elephantine ballet in their
elephantine movements to an
elephantine orchestra. She has
    her
comical tragedies, which
she does not believe
to be entertaining.
She does not seek
    her
love, for she knows that
    her
love may be seeking
    her.
She has
    her
pine tree friends to smoke

cigarettes with, rolling cigars
with their own leaves, and
kicking dogs
as they pass.
she has
     her
experience with a pilgrimage
of accidental accentual alliteration.
she has
     her
ability to disrupt
the tidal activities of a room
that she has never been in, and
she has
     her
capacity to realize that
everybody
is talking about
nothing, and she can do better
than they.
She hangs
     her
skeletons from lampposts in the street light,
and chases skunks into
     her
birthday pond of one leaved houses.
She has
     her
spare sofa parking place, and
     her
rabble-rousing roosters
with their rifftaff riots
to tell
     her
when to crow,
and when to put the sun away.
She has
     her

15

emperor and
    her
bowls empty
with spaghetti.
she has
    her
poetry, unwritten without words
and made of wall paper fruit.
She knows that
    her
reality depends upon
    her
imagination, and she knows
that she has to keep in
    her
mind mush,
that objects can become
more organized than before.
She has
    her
farness from divinity and eternity,
but a realness in privacy.
She has
    her
unawareness of what she will
say next and
    her
eleven days of waiting
until exposing
    her
suppositions of Madagascar, and
    her
contempt for
five seconds ago.
She knew
    her
messiah, before
she ever saw him in

her
walnut waltz or
her
beaded ballad
of a sleepwalking mallard.
She has
her
abundance of lack
of too much, and she
will always take what she is not given.
She makes
me
aware that:
I
miss my galactic isolation, and
I
miss my loneliness.

While

A thunderous silence storms outside of my
thin walled, blanketed tent
While
I lay sedentary in an environment saturated
with murky, unannounced violence
While
A gently whispering, whining wind complains endlessly
to my attentive, listening ear
While
Broken, meaningless thoughts disturb my conditioned sleep
While
A constantly frozen, glaring glance seeps through
my open, unfiltered window
While
My heavily congested head rests uncomfortably
on a sandy, rock pillow
While
I rot as motionless as a linen wrapped mummy
in an isolated sarcophagus
While
Voices inscribe jittery, scrawling, foreign
languages on my slatted forehead
While
Music lectures thoughtful, truthful symbolism that
seems directed towards my confused state of emotion
While
I am brought to wish I where a musician singing of
nonsense that holds the realities of my life, and are
truths to those who listen carefully
While
Emotion builds in my drought stricken eye and spills
onto my dry, desert cheek one lonely droplet at a time
While
I am comforted by the empty, stagnant dark sky that
hides the sun from my shy, sensitive skin

While
Complete strands of words come difficultly to my
pillow eaten, straining soul
While
An internal guidance directs my carnival atmosphere
While
A precise exactness pinpoints the location of myself
on a dusty, thoughtful timepiece
While
The sound of motion destroys my lingering,
tired, fleeing concentration
While
An airy, cotton stuffed twitch violates a deep,
wakeful, nocturnal, considerate drowsiness
While
A slinky, four legged sincerity creeps sneakingly
through a carpeted, jungle floor to my barren bed
of confiscated, coagulated, congested disorder
While
A warm chill beckons the end of a lengthy, difficult search
While
Peace and contentment finalize a seizing tranquility
of stated, contradicting missions
While . . .

Portrait of a Madman

The world's life continues to breath
and move about, even though
I find my life comfortably locked
inside a dark, solitary room
illuminated only by the slanderous
light of a tired, and weak candle.
My life seems to be a myriad of lies
and bullshit occasionally
whispered into my ear
by a gentle, alcohol stained voice.
I find myself cemented
in misuse and misunderstanding.
I find that I often set out to write down
my thoughts in a poetical medium
and end up asking a piece of paper
to fix my life and quiet my hurt.
It seems that every brilliant poet
or author has spent some time
in an insane asylum,
or has decided to discontinue
their lives with a carefully placed bullet.
Or they have drowned in their own sorrow-
filled life; is this because they spent all of their time writing
their mind out of their heads and storing it
in lost and seldom read books and volumes?
Or was it because
they were so disturbingly brilliant
that no one could possibly comprehend
and attain the level of cognition that they contained, and
therefore these geniuses found themselves labeled as loony?
Or is it that the pain and hurt of all the world rests
in the few that
can capably contain and bare it?
I find myself wanting to be locked in a dark room.
I find myself wanting to be a candle,

and locked in a dark room.
I find myself wanting to be the match,
that lights the waxy candle,
that is locked away in a dark room.
I find myself wanting to be me,
but having trouble doing so
without worrying someone.
I find my mind running out
onto this page and I hear a distant candle
calling from a distant asylum room.

When I Fell

I fell from the sky
one cloudless and stormy night
broken winged, and spear wounded.
Lightning fireworks
crashed rhythmically
like the eccentric clacking of passing trains
on cold tracks.
The air was invisible red
and tired of being alone.
I fell from the sky
broken speared, wounded wing
one skyless and tormented night.
Clouds clashed and mangled
rhythmic clackings
of passing trains.
When I fell from the spear winged
broken, wounded sky,
I was a firework train
of eccentric clacking lightning.
The sky was alone red
and tired of being invisible.
I was there
when I fell from the sky
on that trainless and passing night.
The eccentric was cold and clacking tracks.
I was spearwounded
by fireworks and clacking lightning
when I skyed from the fell
in a light sky full of night
and clackings passed eccentric train spears.
The red was sky,
and tired was alone.
You see,
I say,
I saw

a fall of trains
from the works
of lights and fire spears
that broke wings and minds
of eccentric nights that stormed rhythmically.
When I fell from the clacking train
I was a sky of eccentirc fireworks
that speared lightning.
I was a night train
that speared the eccentric sky
like lightning fireworks and wounded clackings.
I was tired and alone
like the red, invisible sky
when I fell.
When I fell
I was lightning.
I was lightning
when I fell
from the skyless night.

In Contemplation of You
(For Zams)

Lost by you foiled around you
insinuations of you
a triumvirate of notations upon you
masculine about you
a religion of you led by you needle of you created for you
music seeing you hearing you spreading wrapping
sneaking and speaking about needing you
lost and excluded from you necessarily you
a new you running and pushing against you
failure of you failing and falling hailing snow bombs
about you chilling you
ending and enlightening you led wandering
spiraling and holding you up against the ceiling of you
robbing and caring for the absence diminishing
and chauffeuring you
faithless faith of you
the squared circle of you arrowed directionally
around the diamond of you
whispered mummers left clinging and clothed thickly around you
watermelons sad about the disappearance of you
eternity and captured crocodiles trailing stairs of you
spliced dissected and dispersed into the atmosphere of you
you creating enumerations of ideas about trapped you
repeated conquests and stipulations of you
you smelling the smiling smiles of you
changing lost into loser of the champions of reciprocal visions
of myths pictured lightly in the rivals of the majesty of you
writing neverendlessly pleasing you pushed by profanity and
spilled ice cream piles of you
planted in seeds of harmony on crossed bridges spanning
the height and width of the weight of you
weighted returning scattered you seething in particles of
your breath left behind you
glimpses of moments of you about you without the childless

fantasies of mispaired and kicked over you
stacked upon you stacked ontop of you
stop
you are too far to be you
stop me
stop you
stop us from being you
wanting you wanting to discherish the thought of refining you
contradictions reciprocating reparations unpaid toward
the future repair of you
taxi cars hailing you lost to you put out on the floor of you
climbing over reverberating pillows
and vibrations of you
traveling through the sun tanned sun dried and poisoned intellect
that is not you
retrieving and hunting the you inside of me
extracting pillar monoliths of worshiping geysers and dancing
painted gypsies inspired by you
reposed reprinted visions incorrect about you wanting
to want to want you hours spent in contemplation of you
the eclectic neon suddenness of you illuminating
the hovering seashells washed clean by waves of
moonlight of you freeingly naked infront of the idea of you
naked thoughts about you reshirted and lying piled in
laundry smells waiting for the arrival of you
softly slithering slinking shinning swinging swimming in
the sleep of you solid delight in the awakening of you
unpaid and striking touches of you harnessed
and collected from you
minuscule pasts conglomerated and devising assorted
arrangements cluttered in the pretext of you
labeled contents of you listing me enlisting me in the army of me
only to purge me from you
by losing the meaning of you
overraising ideologies and politics of you
becoming the prologue to me
avoiding the starlight seeping out of you

unstricken matches burnt out of you
uprooted hills of you enjammbed denominations devoted to you
you walking away from me
walking around me
circling and circling and circling me encircling
the bivouacked encampment of me
daylight daylit daily of you enclosed about me
daylight daylight daylight
closed doors of me seeking you seeing you in the you of me
me in me you in me
repronouncing me depronouncing denouncing me announcing you
receiving you justifying you
nervousness for you in the tendons of me
she displaced me she brightens me she lightens me
tieing anklets of her to me
shackled doorknobs of me executing me unemploying me
writing me out on her word for word
making me into her making me into a blur
you bearing the bearer of you
you conscious of the spark within you
speaking in tongues of you
handling with delicate ease the snakes of me
assassination attempts of the (subconscious) me
footnoted in you
the hallowed halls of me decorated with you
the arsenic arson of you flaming inflaming me
burning inside me burning me
you enflame me
the humiliation of payrolls of loans lent out to me
borrowed from you borrowing you paying the
interest of you trying to secure you
obscured to see me
blue to be me
dragons wadding in the mist of me I mist being you
escaping phone calls of you waking retaliations of you
awkward me in front of you packaged
and displayed to please you in the window of me
the relentless returning of me the reemergence of me

governmental emergency of mental me thinking me
into the existence of you
upon the insistence of you guilting me
the establishment of me
rabid rabbits of me multiplying for you
complex complications of contemplations of you
contingent on you loud about you
disallowed around you round upon you
solidifying you into the (subconscious) me
parenthetical me . . . . me . . . . (me)
me dancing for you dancing around you
dancing to hound you me wrapped up about you
shaped after you
noisily drinking the wine of being beside you
writing a poem about you for you
pictorial depictions of the theoretical hypothesis
of you theorizing you
theorized you replenishing you participating in you
treaties signed over the formation and dividations of you
future plans of you designating you
to the resignation of you
the absolute meaning of you halted by you
repetitions of you repeating you repeating you
repeating you repeating you
holy you in the nocturnal supermarket of you
built to display you
you minimizing me limitating me
the demilitarization of you dezoning you
lost in the middle of you wandering around you
wandering about you wondering about you
wondering around you resoundingly like you
the impossible appeasement of you
the reading of the list of ingredients of you
mixing the mixture of you mixed up about you
cooking in honor of you
the sacrificial sacrifice sufficing me delighting me
the world impressed by you impossible around you
the world enamored with you

the world living inside the palace of you
the false space of me deplenishing me putting an end to me
turning leaflets of me turning me (returning)
leafing me pressing me folding and rebinding me
in the glorification of you
restated stratifications of you cross layered
highlighted symbolic gestures of you
children named after you told to be like you
wanting to be you children's games based on
uncollected (subconcious) you recollecting me salvaging me
the exploring of you the haunting of you
planted by flowers of you blooming and comfortable
with you mutating into you
one hour from the recording of the resolutions
per minute the revolutions per second of you
the revelation of you the karmic resurrection of you
the reincarnation into you the doubling of the
existence of you pursuing the revitalization of me
the raiding and plundering of the (subconscious)
autocracy of you
automatically you
expounding ontop of you abducting you sleeping steadily
beside you in the deciduous arms of you
deciding and describing reciting me exciting me
extracting and imagining me and you never wearing you out.

Never

Once more and I shall never see you again-the length of you
extending into eternity-and me not there to witness you-
your own level of interpretation-   fading away from me-
fading out of vision-I have never heard you say my name
(you might not have know it), I have never said your name aloud-

that may never be otherwise-
I have never actually experienced you, only witnessed,
watched, wanted-wanting wearing away,
eroding slowly in front of you,
without your noticing, without any notice-
dressed, impressed, depressed, and fading away delicately and
indeterminately-
I am red, you are purplish, I write, you read-
what is this locust in my mind?
What forced you to stir so strongly?
Why must I muster a resistance?

This room in which we live (you and I),
seems to resist and conflict with itself-against itself,
I seem to conflict with this room, that is conflicting
with you, who is conflicting with me-
a confliction of fate-an inversion of size, formation,
meaning, will, purpose, power, place-
have we no place to come back to?-
No ground of equalized temperaments?

Never again shall we lose interest with the ghosts of each other.
Never again shall we imagine what was not. Never shall we be.
Never shall we divine each other-I can not stop being inspired
by you-
I shall shadow you until the day that I can no longer stand
to be so close to you without touching you,
and without you ever speaking my name-

Self-Portrait in Green

I am the tragic King,
a man of trivial surrenders
and inspiring violence.
A man who often hears the harsh crash
of splintered violins and passing trains
in the silentest of darkening winds.
Tables shake when I speak,
not from fright but wonder.
I have a smell
similar to that of eaten popcorn
and I often bite softly upon withering rainbows
and ancient books.
When I smile, no one listens,
and when I sneeze no one cares.
I have shocks of wavy knowledge
that I remove like a hat.
I force rain to squeak loudly and lowly
by sitting on top of it; this is a sound that I enjoy.
My eyes have the seeming of a few moments of Zen,
that flee when noticed and reappear in the dark.
I often play with shadowy demons
that lurk in the invisible corners of my midnight room;
we lurk together.
I talk to bugs,
and give names to trees.
In September, I remember
that curbs I could do without.
I am the tragic King,
a man with depressing knees and
flailing elbows.
I find pleasure in my brief moments of insanity,
that leave me seeking cheese flowers for hours.
I grow in strange places,
and long for drying rakes.
I pull hair from the ground,

and throw leaves upon the porches of aging seasons.
I am the tragic King,
weary of peace and strong as battle.
I hunt for roaming looks
and kill them with my thoughts.
I shout the lie of freedom
to innocent strangers,
destroying their prophecies.
I spend my time with bacon spears,
helping them to lose weight
by feeding them fern sticks and shrimp legs.
My skin is the color of leprosy
and my fingernails are brown and scaly.
My back has large knots like wood
and I tie branches around my wrists.
I am the tragic King;
lover of skyward pearls,
and eater of Canadian currency.
I often spend time in Egypt
with my brother the Sphinx,
then visit my Grandfather's goose
in Greece.
I am the tragic King;
dead in the womb.
I am the tragic King,
gave birth to the swimming snake.
I am the tragic King,
executioner for the sick minded.
I am the tragic King,
singer of Brandy Wine.
I am
the tragic King,
and you
do not want
to go where
I am going.

Ceaseless Couch

An empty dusty couch,
situated in an empty, dusty foyer:
endless and unhappy.
How did this couch become so forlorned?
An empty couch, dreaming couch dreams
of walking people, walking by, admiring threads.
Oh couch of endless torture,
scream out, call for peace, free yourself
from your own couchfilled grip of inanimateness.
Pick up your settled feet, your bonded feet,
and move yourself to a new foyer of joy.
There are dust prints in your dust,
like newly fallen snow, falling on snow,
covering your couchless face.
There are seasons, couch;
did you know that there are seasons?
Not seasons of effacing emotion,
but actual life and seasons of facefilled emotions.
Poor couch, withered with wear,
have you no friends to bare?
Oh narcissistic, horrible couch,
shouldered in vain,
all too aware of your own pain.
How many termites have you slain?
When will you reveal yourself?
You bastard couch, fatherless whelp,
show your stuffing, monster, fatherless couch,
beaten, dirty, clothed in misuse,
floating forever in emptiness,
pretending to want to be a chair,
wanting to be personal and personable,
personification of haggardness,
epitome of neverliving, destroyer of destiny,
curtain of courtesy, couch of dead shadows,
and couch of souls misplaced;

show your true stuffing, release your wrath,
free your spontaneously sedentary soul,
free your suddenly sedentary soul
torn, wounded couch: keeper of the outrageous
overture, the outrageously orbiting arachnids.
Couch of being, are you the couch at the end of the universe?
Terrible couch, pretending to comprehend being,
saying: nothing, wearing: nothing, couch, relive your stories,
revive your stories,
whore couch: shredder of saints, father of the fatherless,
fatherless couch, prospector of pain, filth, and torment.
Couch, you are empty, without companions.
Couch, you were seen, starving yourself,
fasting at the feast of love, broken armed, broken legged.
Couch of kings, you are
tarnished with dust and unuse, tarnished with termite feces,
tarnished with termite teeth, toothless, loveless, thoughtless,
empty without companion, taking short cuts to eternity;
couch for no one, situated in an empty foyer,
crowded with: nothing.
A dust riddled couch, praying for people:
couch of vanity and disease.
Stretch yourself couch, become what you cannot be,
be more than any couch has ever been,
be comfortable, be bliss,
couch, touch all walls, floors, and ceilings,
encompass embrace, embrace everything,
seek knowledge of other couches,
direct other couches, walk stairs by yourself.
Damn couch,
harmful harvenger of hags,
scavenger of rags;
suffer you bastard couch,
care not for yourself,
tear out your stitches,
take off your dirty clothes,
and walk away from your empty foyer: your lair of lust;
destroy yourself in sunshine, pinken your pain,

33

you damn couch, believe in daylight,
relive your day's light, trust yourself,
trust another couch, remove your rust,
push down all trespassers of your conscience;
couch of enemies, couch with many enemies,
couch of friendlessness, rabid couch of rabies,
couch of rabidity, couchless couch,
will-less being, shrouded in sorrow and self worth.
Become a military couch, a couch of endless kings,
knight and preserver of couchly rights,
protect your people, couch, speak for them,
speak to your people, couch, show them the beginning
of freedom; emancipate your empty self,
emancipate your empty brethren
from their empty foyers: crowded with: nothing,
soul-less couch, helpless couch, speak
the language of couches: an old speechless,
couchless language, couchless couch.
Empty couch, empty and void of joy,
void of love, void of companion,
couch monster, beast, monster couch,
killer of moths, craver and collector
of dirt and filth, bathe yourself
wash away the wear of years,
pick your feet up, and go where couches go
when completely unrestricted.
Ceaseless couch, forager of failure,
intuitionless couch; trust your visions couch,
uncouch yourself cow couch spotted stubborn,
empty with wealth of nothingness, crewel, jewel-less
couch: finder of fiction, creator of corruption;
couch hidden in endless lakes of empty, endless foyers
of foreverly false couches.
Liar of truth, companionless couch corrupting itself
with dust. Damn bastard couch, forever pretending
to be a couch indifferent to need, indifferent to necessity,
indifferent to caress, indifferent to success, indifferent
to dirt, indifferent to indifference, indifferent

to be a couch indifferent to need, indifferent to necessity,
indifferent to caress, indifferent to success, indifferent
to dirt, indifferent to indifference, indifferent
to all higher powers, Painful couch,
mired in quagmires of guilt and indifference.
Damn couch: corrupter of the caring,
deserter, creator and forerunner of disaster:
hurricane couch, breathing dirty breaths
of inexistent air, pushing plows of breath
from your dirty covers, you are an insult to the living.
Wailing whistle of wanton wickedness:
couch of destruction: Satan couch,
blunt your horns, remove your resistance
to worth, remove your righteousness,
remove your false regality, remove your
wickedness; you wicked couch, remove
your umbilical attachment to evil - devil
couch, remove yourself from this dirt den
of evil- remorse your self-desecration,
remorse your self-mutilation, remorse
your uncouchesness.
Take out your stuffing,
portray your peaceful self
wearer of other dirty couch's rags
and evil. Where is your couch, couch?
Where do you sit?
Sing your outrageous overture,
play your beautiful sonnets of endless death,
speak your words of useless wisdom:
writer of persistent lust and inadequacy:
inadequate seat of starvation:
writer of wickedness, couch of nails
and rose thorns, covered in wretched wickedness,
pretending to sleep in empty foyers:
keeper of no one's secrets, empty couch
full of emptiness and empty visions of nothing,
disgraced and diligently dirty couch.
Oh ceaseless couch: prophet, monk of filth

and degradation, humiliation, and vanity,
wallowing in vain attempt at immortality,
speaking spiked words void of passion,
void of compassion, void of personality,
void of hunger, void of light, void of height:
secretariat of lewdness and shrewdness,
obliterator of rationality, abstainer of content,
tear out your stuffing, tear down your defenses.
Bastard couch: perverter of pretense,
exterminator of endless shards of reality,
reverberator of eavesdropped conversations
and false insight, mad couch of corrupted mind,
massager of truth, spreader of misconception,
colonel of corruption, matchless arson, flameless fire,
mangler of perception with maimed insight,
wrinkled couch, your worth is wrinkling,
raider of the houses of mouses: moveless mythological monster,
what is your intention?
What is your intended meaning?
What is your intended purpose?
Eight-seven years of mal intent, you couch
of vagabonds, worthless, useless,
decaying, decomposing, covering a dusty foyer
floor with dirt, consorter with Satan, sabotager of safety.
Awful couch, swallowed by seas of graves of extinction,
in love with your loneliness, lonely with: nothing,
reprisal of: nothing, couch of: nothing
god of: nothing, worshiper of: self-despisement,
no meaning, no nothing, writer of rhythmless rhetorical rhetoric,
have you no dignity? Have you no stuffing?
Have you anything underneath your wooden skeleton?
Where is your wooden talisman? Your wooden necklace?
Have you anything to hold you together?
Do you feel whole?
Do you complete yourself?
Allow for some sight, you evil couch.
Allow for some hands, you vile spirit.
Remove your dark sunrise, bathed in black:

evil sunrise. What is your life philosophy,
dirty beast of a couch?
What limits the width of your villainy?
Did you know your dark sun does not exist,
outside the domain of your foyer?
Have you ever been lifted above your own horizon?
Taunt me no more, theologian of thirst,
and discontinue
your mocking of my love
for a tall girl.

Mirror, Mirror

Remember,
Do not let yourself forget
Remember what you felt,
Do not let your memory decay
Remember and retain what you have learned,
Do not let it leave you
Recall what you know,
Do not let your emotions die
Reshape your past,
Do not let it guide you
Replace what hurts you,
Do not let it destroy you
Reharness your energy,
Do not let it consume you
Reestablish your knowledge,
Do not let it control you
Replenish your soft side,
Do not let it expose you
Refine yourself,
Do not let you unravel you
Readministrate your conscience,
Do not let it console you
Recreate your flight,
Do not let yourself ground you
Recollect your patience,
Do not let your angst invade you
Recuperate your chaos,
Do not let order pervade you
Reinvent your style,
Do not let it disguise you
Reconstruct your mentality,
Do not let it displace you.
Rearrange your sanity,
Do not let it unhinge you
Redream your sleep,

Do not let it evade you
Reencompass your ideas,
Do not let them persuade you
Recorrect your voice,
Do not let it escape you
Reapproach your reality,
Do not let it pervert you.

Pay attention to the events
        that you are not able to notice,
Deject those objects
        that are beyond comprehension,
Move your being to a position
        that you are not able to reach,
Align yourself along a continuum
        that halts shorter than what is perceivable,
Ignite the night that shines
        in the morning sunlight,
Play in the crisp leaves that fell
        from the tree roots,
Hide in the artwork
        that disrupts Autumn's Shade,
Realize the importance of imagination
        and materialize your own reality,
Alter your world to fit your perceptions,
        Alter your perceptions to fit your world,
Manifest manifested manifestations
        in order to make sense of sensible sensibility.

Do not pervert your reality,
let it approach you
Do not escape your voice,
let it correct you
Do not persuade your ideas,
let them encompass you
Do not evade your sleep,
let it dream you
Do not unhinge your sanity,

let it arrange you
Do not displace your mentality,
let it construct you
Do not disguise your style,
let it invent you
Do not pervade your chaos,
let order recuperate you
Do not invade your patience,
let angst collect you
Do not ground your flight,
let yourself create
Do not console your conscience,
let it administrate you
Do not unravel yourself,
let you refine you
Do not expose your soft side,
let it replenish you
Do not control your knowledge,
let it establish you
Do not consume your energy,
let it harness you
Do not destroy what hurts,
let it replace you
Do not guide your past,
let it shape you
Do not recall what you know,
let your emotions die
Do not leave what you learned,
let it remember and retain you
Do not remember what you felt,
let your memory decay
Do not forget,
remember yourself.

I Feel as Though I Am Feeling

I feel as though
    I have been shipwrecked, stranded
    on a solitary island
    where my needs will never know any fulfillment.
I feel as though
    it is my interaction with a soffow-filled world,
    that is leaving me to feel sorrow-full.
I feel as though
    my life, my world
    must be changed or it will end
    quickly.
I feel as though
    I accidentally gave away my thunder
    by not carefully selecting who I shared it with.
I feel as though
    I am as absurd as a milk bottle shaped cloud
    in a multilayered, multicoloured horizon.
I feel as though
    the sun would cry
    if the moon fell from the midnight sky.
I feel as though
    repetition halts progress.
I feel as though
    repetition halts progress.
I feel as though
    every dog is not made of tear drops,
    every rain drop is not made of shadows, and
    every window is not made of water vapor.
I feel as though
    poetry can never be restrained,
        and
    every song is not meant to be profound.
I feel as though
    your slogan is a lie,
        and

all of your heroes must die.
I feel as though
    lightning can exist in solitary bursts,
        and
    people do disappear.
I feel as though
    small units of knowledge
        and
    extended thoughts
    need not be iambic.
I feel as though
    my stimuli are being withheld
    and I am slowly wilting
    like a flower growing in nutrientless soil.
I feel as though
    pages are intentionally being ripped from my book
    in order to render my story incomplete and disproportional.
I feel as though
    my future is being foreclosed.
I feel as though
    my mentality is being misformed
        and
    that there is something drastically
    wrong with my mind.
I feel as though
    Satan created love as a means to deprave and downtrod.
I feel as though
    my theory of Planetation is (in)correct.
I feel as though
    my mind is influencing my memories.
I feel as though
    my subconscious poetry is infiltrating
    my yellow saffron writings.
I feel as though
    it is the chaos of society
    that is producing unforgiving change.
I feel as though
    it is the impetuousness of youth

that supplies evolution.
I feel as though
someone ate my soldiers while I was sleeping.
I feel as though
I am writing with my mind closed and my eyes open.
I feel as though
I can no longer comfort and help myself
I feel as though
I have become shipwrecked
on an isolated island
where my needs will never know
any fulfillment.

An Attempt at Removal

A pool of water becomes the container
and not the substance,
the substance does not contain the container;
it is the container that contains the substance,
and therefore the pool is the container;
it is a simple question of duality.
Or rather, the question should be:
Is is the isness of is?
And the obvious answer would be:
Yes, is is the isness of is.
Yet, this is merely a jocundal bravado,
vacillating between inured and inundated.
It is also easily shown and well known,
that it is easier for the protagonist to turn antagonist,
than to push the other shoulder to the other shoulder.
While, it is also known that:
glass is a liquid, that slowly settles
to the bottom of widow panes;
yet, water is not a fast moving glass;
is this an embellishment?
No, this only shows that:
is is really the isness of is.
Then it may be asked:
Can plastic fruit grow from plastic plants?
The only proper reply would be:
Reality, my friend, is everywhere.
As, a poem slowly nods,
like a sleeping God,
dreaming premonitory worlds
and then winking
himself into existence,
like a solitary red star,
in an afternoon sky.
The star is shamed,
and he thinks:

Where is Lazarus?
This causes red, evaporated cockroach dust
to sprinkle onto the earth,
and onto a blindfolded possum,
reading a lightly nodding poem.
The possum believes,
that the river is his fault,
and that he is the salt of that fault.
He drinks in the brown eyes
of the spell of a female possum,
and dresses her in poetry
with his covered and cowarded eyes.
The possum sees himself as an attempt at removal.
Removal of what, he is not sure,
but anyhow, he scurries away
from a winter holocaust,
and the possibility of existence.
To him it is Holy Wednesday,
and he has a head like a catholic cougar
transgressing a crack in a sidewalk.
Although, he has never met
a cougar or a catholic,
and has no notion of a sidewalk.
He eats the plastic fruit that grows
on a plastic plant,
wherever it is that he is sitting,
for he is pleasingly free,
when he suddenly realizes that:
ideas are revolutionary,
no matter how simple they are.
Then he thinks:
is is really the isness of is?
Or, possibly is it that:
is is the isness of isn't?
He is sure that it is.
Or maybe he isn't.
Then, the possum ponders the possibility of
is being the isness of was;

can is be the isness of was?
He sees this as a blooming fancy
of impossibility and ascertains
that he is a blooming fancy
and he himself is an impossibility.
He then realizes that it is all impossible:
a was being an is,
and is wasing a wasn't during an isness
while ising on a wasn't in front of a being.
It is all too confusing
and expanding too rapidly
for his feebleness.
The possum then ponders:
maybe is never was a was and
if was was a was, then is is a was? No, that can not happen:
An is has to was a being,
in order for that is to is
as a was would was
if it were an is.
Now this seems entirely possible;
he is sure of it.
In fact, he says to himself
possum, I am sure of it.
But then, what if it is a was?
Then, would that it be a was
that was an is ising an isness,
or an is that isn't a was,
and was more of a being
being an is so that it could be an it?
What?: The possum thinks.
If it were a was,
it would first have to be an is.
What is is if it cannot be an is?
Is it an isn't?
Or a wasn't?
Only the possum knows.
Or does he?

The Moon and The Concrete

Part I: The Night
I walk slowly, stepping heavily on my sorrows,
and praying softly to the shadowy moon,
who hides behind thin, dark clouds
allowing his light to penetrate their souls.
The demons of the night are present:
in a berry dropping from a distant tree,
in the echoes of my false footsteps,
in the silent stillness, and
in my uneasy heart.

Part II: The Day
I will not have time to live today,
nor will I tomorrow. I feel as though
I might not get out of life alive.
Music is changing my life.
The music in my life is changing.

Part III: Perceptions
I do not want to exist physically anymore;
I want to exist in the important realm,
the realm of ideas and imagination.
I do not want to be seen. I do not want to be touched.
I want to be heard and felt deep within.
I want to be like the moon, or like a finely tuned piano.
I want to be a poem and have my inky blood
permanently stained on paper.
I want to be described with pictures of the midnight sky.

Part IV: Concrete Bridges
A long crudely constructed, concrete bridge
led me to the other side of myself.
A side that only exists in the absence of the moon.
A side that is a wind that gently removes the colored
and dying leaves from a tree.
A wind that forces the leaves to rain down
and cover the cold ground.
A long walk away from myself, I found me hiding

in a darkened park.
A bridge made of concrete helped me to destroy myself

Part V: The Imaginary Nothing

My sleep always seems to be daringly dreamed.
I often sleep in my walk and swim in the lake above my head.
I talk to the moon and listen to the concrete.
I often get lost in translation and
I often interpose myself with my poetic alter-ego.
Ambiguousness and ambivalence are my only debauched and disingenuous friends.
I am cemented in The Moon and in The Concrete.

Money

You are a liar, money
money, where is my money? money
money, you are turning black
money, I do not want to be with you anymore, money
money, leave me alone, money
money, I can not stand your constant calls, money
money, stop slinking into my bed, money
money, I do not have enough money
    to pay for your money, money
money, you are everywhere, money
money, I can feel you growing in my hair, money
money for Africa
money for the South
money to choke my mouth money
money, you are a lout, money
money, I saw you scampering down the street
  like incandescent eyesight money
moneymoneymoneymoneymoney
money for a monkey
money for a muse
money has no use
money for money
money, you are an insult, money
money for food money
    drug money
    milk money
    stolen money
    hot and cold money
    no money is happy money
money money to repress money
    mental money imagining more money
    sleeping money wrapped in dirty money
money for America
money from America
money is America

honey money
money, you are money's money
   hey money, your face has fallen!
   hey money your price has risen!
money, what do you spend your money on, money?
money, do I have your attention, money?
money, I burnt your money
money, do you exist today?
money, I gave all of my money to St. Peter's money
money, I turned your woman into a rabbit money
money, four minus eleven equals negative money
money, admit that it was you that stole
   the apple from the snake money
money, you are not the perfect professor, money
money, more minds make more money
money, I refuse to listen to your bleeding remarks, money
money, you are not as abstract as you want to be, money
money, do you remember all of your children?
money, do not pretend to be indifferent
money, I saw you in Viet Nam, money
money, how many languages do you speak now?
money is Custer still standing in your fault money?
money, do you still live in a house of ecstasy and money?
Money Mouse?
money, you are not worth my money
money, I will give you everything that is inside me,
      but it will most likely crush you, money
money, you murderer, I know that it was you
   who killed Einstein, money
money, I hope that you kill yourself, money
money, I will not pay for the faults of my father, money
money, you are not the master race, money
money, I will not let you exterminate me again, money
money, you are not a national masturbation, money
money, you sold out to your money, money
money, you are a fascist orgy and a dictator, money
money, you have more worth, money, as a tree, money
money, you are a liar!

Sunny as Marmalade

"May she sheep with knife needles," said Satan
to the Marmoset's fight of forage.
The bright glistening Moon wind
dampened the shadow souls of yellow rock soil,
and "all was sunny as marmalade"
quoted the oven to the diaper thief.

Just then a piano chimed nine ninety, and
the Happy Demon delivered apple soup to the Dragon King
and all was sunny as marmalade for today.

The door knocked on the wall, and
the phone spoke deliberately of political pigs
and the satire of milky residues about clocks and vegetables;
while posters of paintings drank slowly from paper fires
and initiated the interpretive dance of the Honeysuckle Eggs.

The sizzle of electric heat explained my failures to myself,
while I imagined my memory
storing external events internally.

Forelorned restraining poetry emasculated
the cultural context of control in one's diminishing sleep.
He is he who is the character of Life.

"Was does not the candle wax grow down
into the belly of dripping sound?" asked the incense to the
Angel Fairy for she was as jolly as the dark lining of the world.
She sneezed several orgasm sparks and scratched her
thinking thoughts, then flopped her teeth

to her cheshire lips, "suffer not,
ye child of newly mistaken births. Thy chord of
harmonic device speaks loudly
of climbing rain violins and singing frogs
of lasting death. Rise and Demise!"
She shrieked as she broke into athousand shards of hate
and spilled across the wall of knowledge.

The future will change similar tasks
into plastic paper of unequivocal dismay,
for the Beast of Festivities is a friend
of fragrant flowers and the bluest of purple skies.
For if you change your life, you change your world
and all of its transgressions.
And, all can be sunny as marmalade.

The Pumpkinseed House lies
beyond the Fallen Forest of Extinguished Kitten Breath
along the bread of salt that tastes more of ash
than horse sweaters.
"Beware the heart of the Bamboo Snake," warns the Crow thrice
over his shoulder from the peak of the rain cellar stairs.

The moon laughed at the reflection of myself
through his silent, silvery red eyes
between the blades of grass pasted to the ends of rabbit branches;
while the obese Life Eater begged to be fed (and he shall).

For itis the mind of thoughts, that holds the blackberry bush
disgruntled and whimsical;
for itis the pain of remembrance that dooms the forgetful
toad to dislodge his seasons of ripe cherry blossoms
and mud icicles;

For itis the judgement of the eyeless sight that congeals
and provokes visions of illusion and disorder;
for itis the rumors of the savior's suicide
that beckons all from the crystal, cascading city of wonderment.

The magic pumpernickel coins display the
smokey breath of ghosts,
and their melancholia distorts and divides their attack
upon the realm of dementia and imaginary spells.

The bitter infusion of infiltration and hopes of holocaust
cause misshapen breath from the Jack of Spades
and bruises revealing coagulation
plus the sorrow of sad sucklings shifts sweetly
towards sorrow and sadness
and will never be sunny as marmalade.

Permeable power titans summon creative, fanciful sorcerers;
while retrospective butterflies scatter
faces across several eons of districts of shells
that have washed up upon the Heaven's shelves
melting muses and instruments
of assorted colours and uses.

Air interacts with thought particle collisions
and speech infers nonsense in the feet of shoe weasels
and worm beads.

The Arboreal Hypothesis of chipmunks
and moles circle birds of azure leaves and platinum hopes
with waves of referential wisdom
and suspended falsehoods.

Jewels release water vapor of fear and wishes,
doubts of splendor and the laughter of tears,
while splicing tendons of relief into ribbons of despair
and valleys of fortitude.

If the sunny marmalade were actually a cup of language,
a burrow of bloody constellations may impact would be vitamins
of chocolate and yellow hurts made of black butter bagels
caught on branches of distrust and disbelief.

To believe, is to taste the sweetness of lemon coughs
or the insult of rhubarb termites.
In such a case,
the all can never be marmalade as the Sun
and the ground of invisibility will disappear
into the catastrophes of polliwogs.

Small mushrooms of triumph push daisies of delusion
into swirls of poppy spinach
and the squirrels of delight relinquish
in the confusion of conformity causing
the corrosion of disfaithful fathers
and sisters of motherly love to argue
that flesh furthers the journey of November carts
and wooden spikes build the lights into passing bridges.

But as for today,
tonight,
but not the last week of right now
all is sunny as marmalade
and the contentment of relief is elating
and comforting, for the Thinker of Grandiose Thoughts
enjoys his moments of truth
and his efforts reveal themselves to himself

as he whistles that
all is indeed sunny as marmalade.

Solar Powered Dedications

I
The musical light strikes the parched ground
with heaping sympathy, as
the image represented in the glossy stare of the mirror
mirrors, mocks, and laughs glossily at his real self
While The Rodents of Self Defeat enter your brain
with returning despair
and feed upon your impaled, poisoned thoughts;
Death is coming, and I am slowly dying.
By a chilling fireside, which is burning
on the ashes of a dozen other dead poets,
I sit with the Walker of Eucalyptus Nights, talking
about how we are dampened by the shadow
of the howling Moon.

II
The mental race has begun;
stockpile your thoughts in brain burrows
as a means to barricade memories
for reasons of self defense and internal insanity.
The Atlas to my eternal Soul has been recovered.
It outlines every road to my body's Capital,
every geographic scope is referenced to in depression marks.

III
Shave my teeth when I die;
I do not want my Mother to see them,
lying besides me in my coffin.
Before she comes to my funeral,
peel the layers of snail sludge off of the antique furniture
that I borrowed from Grandmother's den; the same furniture
that she peeled sludge from only ten years before.
Warn her of the worms that haunt the kitchen
and stole from the barren cupboards
while I was sliding bare chested on the recently marred floor.

56

Remove from my grip the hair that I purchased
from the broken pencil lead seller
after murdering him with the small, useless ball of lint
that was in the bottom of my coat pocket.

IV
Tell my Mother
about the travesty of traffic violations,
and the corruptness of slender sidewalks,
soaking in their own wealth of handkerchief dirt.
Tell my Mother
how large kites flew about my head
and tickled the fancies of my thoughts
while I carefully and diligently digested the laudanum
of false histories and slivers of the present future.
Tell her.
Tell her how the Bandits of Truth vacated
the vacant Building of Honesty
by shouting obscenities at the pigeons of poor luck.
Tell her of the torn and soiled cardboard sheets
that covered me while I slept.
Tell my Mother
how you found me wandering around brick streets
on my knees screaming at a delusional squirrel
for stealing my pork chops.
Tell her about my homeless friends
who rummaged through rusty garbage cans
for discarded clothing for me to wear in the winter.
Tell her of the permeating stench of blatant illiteracy
that stained my arms and neck.
Tell her.
Tell her how I smashed the boundaries of today
when I put my fingers through the legs of my towel
and pretended that I was President of the Marshmallow birds.
Let my Mother know
about the lumps of cornbread that left across the Arctic
with my stomach snakes and my pictures of dogs paws.
Tell her about the time

57

that I danced on the bathroom tile
singing to the shower curtain and
how I thought the light bulb was jealous
of my affair with the shaving cream.
Tell her. She needs to know.
Tell my Mother
that I chased the spying Dragonfly
out of the fifth story window
of the briar patch that was in the northeast
corner of my hotel room.
Tell my mother
that my bruised ego was due to the demon
who haunts my room at night
and passes me pornographic pictures through the wall.
Tell my mother.
Tell her.
Tell my mother how I grasped the purpose of Carpet Mice,
and tell her the truth about how
when no one else would, I grasped my own hand.

The First Night
of Summer

It is the first night of Summer and
I have been given the power of rhythm,
I have the power of rhyme,
I have knowledge of the fact
that your heart is tailored to fit mine
and my soul is tailored to fit yours,
and yet I hang,
unworn,
in your closet of abandonment.
My life on a match head,
about to be scraped across sandpaper;
your life the stick;
without you,
I have no where left to fit;
I have nothing left to write,
nothing left to say (please stay),
please come to here
my dear,
come and play near.
Instead, you chew me into small bits,
and help me to imagine myself as real,
but I still question whether I will matter
when I run out of words
(As I already have). I cannot write;
my words are too honest-too clear
(yet, I must write until my writing returns).
Patience,
relax,
we have our whole next life time to write poems into each other,
our whole next life time to write each other into poems.
It is because of you that I am like me,
now that I have the power to conjure
my imagination in my fist like a swirling marble,
(I believe that you have seen me more bold that this.)

59

You give me order, I give you disorder,
I give you the flame at the end of a candle,
lit with my mind and decorated with a daisy;
I give you speech, you give me reach,
and then tell me where to end
(if I am the beginning, then you will never cease).
Watch me duck,
I will watch you dive,
it is for you that I have arrived,
and now it is all your fault that I am real,
you have made me an ex-convict of myself.
I read you, absorb you, and write everything in your name,
inspired in your omnipresence; because of you
I have wasted my reason
and now I feel as though I am a week away from you,
I am a week behind you.
I stand underneath you, and you raise me above myself, and
force me to see that I am real.
I try to lean against you, but instead lean through you;
you foreshadow me where
I used to come before my shadow
(shadow, black shadow of night);
I can only turn your page over to the blankside,
I can only turn away from you now (now I am inside),
I seem to halve you
when I read you,
when I need you
to prove to me that I am real (you whole me).
You continue to fill page after page after page of poetry
that I am unable to write,
you are the unwriteable poem that I have been trying to recreate
for the past month now; you crash over me like words
I cannot write, you splash over me like words
that I do not know, words that I cannot write fill you,
fill over you
until all that is left of you remains inside of me (where I am).
Every morning I wake up in a bed of blues,
your angel wing soft lips pressed against mine and captured, held

by my imagination (like a swirling marble in my fist).
There is a thick grey fog settling around me like a crowd,
losing me in the midst of the middle of the mist,
in an unseeable cover, in an unseeable corner of my insanity;
you make me want to grow old,
and I refuse to feel guilty about missing you;
I refuse to keep my persuasion factor down,
I chose to keep my composure around,
but I cannot understand why the moon becomes more visible
as I walk towards it, I cannot understand why I believe
that I would scrape the softness off of your face
with the caress of my palm, I cannot understand why
you seem so outwardly cloudy and why I feel
so inwardly cloudy, I cannot understand why
I feel lost in you, when I can still see
the edges of you, I cannot understand why
I continue to remain a week away from knowing
the absolute meaning of you, I cannot understand why
my handwriting keeps changing,
I cannot understand why I am a full hour and a half away
from talking with anyone, I cannot understand
why I never know when it is going to rain thoughts
in my drought-stricken mind,
I cannot understand why your mind is not extending
into mine or why my mind is not extending into the moon,
I cannot understand why my favorite roads are so far away
from my destination, I cannot understand why
my slope is so horrendous, or why I am left to dance
with your shadow, long after you have left, I cannot understand
why I am so undirectionally based,
or why you never turn around
when I think about you, I cannot understand why
each event has to have its own line
or why no one hears me even when I write loudly,
I cannot understand why I am more afraid
of the things that I do know,
I cannot understand why I always progress too far,
I cannot understand why I cannot understand

everything that I say, I cannot understand why I cannot
swirl in your fist, I cannot understand why
you are a sunny setting, cloudlessly, rainy day
or what caused some of me to fall down
(come over to hear my dear, come and play near),
I do not understand why I can see by the moonlight
how large my pupils have grown.
I can hear cars chased away into obscurity,
I can see me standing
in front of the motorcycle headlight of the moon,
I can see the universe swirling
into the absolute insanity of nothingness,
I can see every digital molecule of the breeze, floating,
drifting across the brilliant gravity of the moon as it beams
your shadow across rooftops,
and yanks people out of their churchpew houses
and into the punch-hole presence of the moon,
I can feel the pretentious moon pretending
to be my personal planet, looking down at me
with one Kyklops eye;
the large mouth of the moon is swallowing the whole sky
and swallowing me whole;
the pistachio nut scrapings of my mind are scattered sparsely
around in the moon bright, along with imagined fellowships
of sound and memory,
and yet, there is not one of we amoung us;
while, as for me,
I can only continue to be,
on this warm Summer's eve
(and still, I may not be here when I leave).
I would trade all of my bliss
for just one kiss
from the moonlight,
if only you would come and play here
my dear,
come and play near
the hope restored by the glaring moon who is a spectacle
of itself, spectacular to itself,

come and play near me, while I am still only
a staircase away from a moonwalk,
or sitting on the rooftop of the moon,
frozen in extraterrestrial glow,
pondering nothingness, the moon has become
momentarily uncreated,
and reality invaded with the intensity of the steady pulse
of electric moon bright;
the vacant air rainbow of midnight
is being crushed by complexity,
and replaced with a new sense of partiality, a biting sense
of the diminishing fog,
replaced with the retreating sensibility of the future;
the unwatched televisions of reality are all muted
and disregarded for the rudimentary religion of music,
and followed by the sound of ministry in dripping
faucets of failure, echoing
in bleached hallways of moonlight;
I am blatantly fixated with returning, shaking, quaking,
speechfilled nightmares of moonlight,
intensified by the moon bright;
there are walking myths of nothingness curling around the spine
of the moon shine,
portraying remembered holidays from sadness,
that are still and always a long way away from
the absolute insanity of midnight
as it fractures into impossible colours of clear,
viscous liquid, fluid with feeling.
I have been kicked off of the couch of frustration,
and like a dog, fed the sour bone of sleepwalked fears;
the absolute meaning of the moon is parked
at the station of inconceivability;
moved about angles of perception
of possible moonlight are shinning
in the encompassing abandonment of midnight,
while the confessional laboratory of moonlight continues
to be haunted by phantom's footsteps, who stamp footprints
in the ferocity of the moon's light; the moon is hiding

nothingness, hiding more than nothingness,
hiding a nothingness without a name (nothing too descriptive),
hiding sleeping rumors of moon shadow, of moon shade,
and burying small, chewed bits of me in the backyard
of the moonlight; midnight is gasping and choking
on the moon bright, while moonlight
pours out of sleeping mouths like a cool breeze
of actuality with strange fleeting noises of security
that are shadowed by the movement of the moon;
the darkside of the moon is shinning
an aura, that is presenting the soul of the moon,
and directing the orchestra of the sky;
the large open bed of midnight (like my bed of blues),
is unslept in, sheeted, and defeated;
glancing, insistent footsteps inspired by delusions,
are now left with no place to sleep but the floor
of reversed reality,
awake until the moon has begun retreating,
the daylight repeating itself for inexistent no one
(a double negative of reality);
my past is sitting in a mocking chair situated
near to the city of madness,
and bringing me to wonder why I can not understand why
I traveled two hundred and forty miles at eighty miles an hour
with thoughts of you at every turn of the odometer
without considering that you would not want to be me,
I never considered that I would be twisting and turning
like the night,
that I would be twisting and turning in the night
(please, please come
play near
my dear,
come and play near);
I never considered that the absolute meaning of midnight
had to be segregated
from the concept of the sun;
there is now hair blowing in my face,
blowing my cares into waste,

and my long drive away from you is being mentally retraced,
my security misplaced, my dignity replaced, my meaning erased
and clouded like a school of fish swimming in the wavy sky,
lost and murdered in a field of rye;
I am driving through the shadows of clouds
cast by the covered sun
and dodging meteorite showers of you
is like escaping
the clenching jaws of a cloud alligator like a wingless,
wounded bird
(I am sure that I have fallen off of your sidewalk again);
for now, it seems, that
you bury your pleasure where it will not be found,
when all that I want is to add to your riches,
but I do not believe that you will ever come
my dear,
I do not believe that you will ever come
and play near to here,
but I still wish for you
to restrain the moonlight
with your reality,
so that I may continue
to be real.

Walking Walls:
An Experiment in Disorientation

A lon
g, nar
row h
allw
ay: a hun
dred yar
ds lon
g, fou
r fee
t wid
e, an
d fou
r fe
et hig
h a
nd bat
hed wh
ite. A lar
ge blu
rred o
bjec
t at th
e fa
r en
d. A fig
ure o
f und
eterm
inable s
ex, hei
ght, len
gth, co
lor, ma
ss. Slo

wly
s
o
m
er
sa
ul
t
i
ng
to
ward
the o
bje
ct a
t th
e
end.
Whe
n it reac
hes t
he o
bj
ect, it col
lap
ses
in ex
haust
ion, an
d un
bal
ance.
Loo
king u
p thro
ugh un
cal
ibrat

ed eyes,
th
e fig
ure rea
lize
s tha
t th
e obj
ect
is
a th
rone.
Th
e thro
ne is
cru
del
y cons
truct
ed o
f woo
den fen
ce pos
ts an
d dou
ble en
ded nai
ls. Th
en,
fro
m th
e posi
tion wh
ere th
e figu
re ha
d begu
n, a coff

in round
s an in
exis
tent corn
er,
pus
hed b
y a
n invis
ible coron
er. Th
e coff
in ap
proa
ches slo
wly, sli
ding
alon
g th
e slic
k soi
l of
th
e hal
lwa
y. An
d th
e fig
ure dis
ap
pear
s int
o th
e wal
king wa
lls . . .

Two Heartbeats, The Rain, and Two Candles

Part One: The Sound of Heartbeats

heart
heart
beat
heart
beat
heart beat
The sun is going down
to rest
exhausted from a long day
of staring at the Earth,
heart beat
the sky is darkening
with clouds,
The rhythm of the world
in a
heart beat
the rhythm of Nature
is a
heart
beating
heart beat
heart beat
one golden, chocolate heart
beating
against another
heart beat
my life
beating
at an encompassingly steady pace,
one
two
heart
beat
you beating

my heart
at a steady race,
I can feel you beating
your heart
from as far
away as you are
heart
beat
heart
I can hear your heart
beating
down rain
on my
heart beat
one two
heart beat
I can feel your heart
beating
down rain
on my heart;
the sun has gone down
and taken his
heart beat
down with him,
your sky is still beating,
your heart pumping kindness
through the atmosphere,
through my atmosphere
heart beat
heart beat
slow beat
steady beat
I watch for your heart
beat
with stellar speculations,
or carried by wind drifts
and drafts
steady

one two
heart beat
(Does your
heart
beat
for me,
as my
heart
beat
is for you?)

Part Two: The Meaning of Rain

I have spent much time with myself
this summer,
but I have never felt lonely,
never, not once;
I always felt you with me;
I kept you with me,
in my mind,
all of you
with me;
you have a part in every aspect
that is me, all of me, always;
it is raining here tonight;
you are here, and you love this glossy rain;

I know now that it is raining, that
you are the rain,
you are reminded by the rain,
you are forcing me to remember the rain;
I see you smiling in each raindrop, smiling at each raindrop,
and every drop kissing my skin
and then traced away gently;
I am caught in you;
and you thunder,
like a jet plane racing the sky;
you open my mind and let me out;

I wonder if you are raining
where you actually are,
right here and now you are raining inside me,
you are raining all over me, for
you are as beautiful as your description,
your depiction of the rain;
I want to ask you long distance questions
with my thoughts at
close distances,
I want to feel,
the rain of you,
the rain inside you;

It is raining here,
and your letter,
your poem just arrived
just before the rain came;
the rain sent with your letter,
the rain dependent upon your poem,
you and I independently dependent
on the rain;
Did you intend for this to happen?

(Did you intend for us
to happen?)
Now it seems that
all that I can do is wait
for anyday
to come

Part Three: Two Candles Melting

I have time spent with myself,
burning away like a candle,
sealing over memories and inspiration;
comfortable with concealment,
cozy inside closed doors,
shut away from reality,

and waiting for the candle
waiting elsewhere,
two hundreds of miles away;
forced apart
by time,
comfortable with concealment,
cozy inside closed doors,
and shut
away from reality;
there is no pain
transpiring,
no hurt rising
with the horizon,
I am wishing on a feeling,
painted with dripping wax,
painted with wishes and dreams,
and hopes for a melding mixture,
a conglomeration of candles
melting together;
burning flames of midnight
are slowly roasting the moon
as it rises
with you;
flickering candle stars
removed from the horizon
resembling two candles shut apart,
two hundreds of millions of miles away
from melting,
from reviving;
life times away,
only memories to stay,
only burning for anyday;
two candles unable to stare,
at two candles, two hundreds of miles away,
my world within me and turning,
my candle for you, slow and burning
at the distance of two hundreds of miles;
pictures of smiles,

painted with lipstick warmness,
sent over two hundreds of miles;
the harder that I think,
the more that I can only remember
the movement of your lips,
the movement of your speech, continuous and steady,
like your storm spreading around me,
spreading above me; I listen
for your gently strummed guitar,
early in the morning, drifting
like pollen through my open window
(me an open window), and you,
you are laughing with the sunrise,
like the two of you were up
together all the last night
that I saw you;
now I see you
dancing with my dreams,
and dripping candle wax wishes
into my mind while I am sleeping
to the sound of your
heartbeat
heart
beat
heart
beat
heart
beat
heart
heart

From Out the Sea

One

She came from out the sea,
bathed in eloquent simplicity,
speaking in gestures
of self correction;
she seems to be a connection
to the disaster occurring in every direction.

She is the Earthquaker,
singing her songs of the Gods
and her conjectures
of her apprehension of ill-reality.

She wants to be more
than she can conceive,
but actually,
she is only what she comprehends.
She is like a failed metaphor
comparing herself.

She thinks . . .
She thinks,
"Does anything have to do
with anything? Or
does everything
stand aside from everything?"

She prefers to stand aside
from anything and everything.

She feels like No one
else.

She feels like someone
else.
She feels like everyone
else.
She feels more like everyone
else
than everyone
else.

She can be described
in tremendous detail
by not being described.
She is like poetry
preventing poetry
through the use
of dissimilar objects,
like the awkward pinkness
of a shy polar bear playing chess
with a brown car in the park
at noon on a Saturday.
She refuses to be a poem.
She refuses to be a poem
used only to fill the pages of a book.

She does not apologize for her knowledge,
for her knowledge is not always wisdom;
she will not conform
to individual conformity.

"Does everything stand aside from everything?"

She falls asleep in forty
unconnected pieces,
like that of lamented cement;
She wishes those pieces to be scattered
in the shadows where she stands.

From where she stands,
she admires randomness
for the no sense of no meaning
of randomness.

Two

From out the darkness,
a gentle breathly whisper
on her face and a gentle
breathly kiss on her ear;
an embrace from the darkness,
an embrace with the darkness.

There are long hairs all about her,
there are long textual caresses
from out her and the circular glimpse
of a soft nipple winking in the night.
A trombone takes flight
with the feathery commotion
of an eye in the blank.

And the darkness . . .
The darkness continues
to bend over her,
like an angel in her sleep.

One becomes two.
Two becomes two ones.
Two ones becomes hope
for oneness.

Three

Her town will become happy again,
one month of love justifies
the wax on the weather, only

she wishes that she had more to say;
She will say more, in time,
when given time.

She held me
when I could not hold myself,
I could not hold myself
but she held me,
And, I held her
when I could not hold myself,
I could not hold myself
but I held her, and
she held me.

Four

She wrote once,
using a tidal title,
of a narrating fish
in an ocean of spikes,
impaled on its own judgement.
She wrote once, of two minds
making two worlds
between themselves,
and these worlds are worlds
that nothing is known about,
they are only known of.

What is the world thinking?
She only knows
what she thinks about
the world;
but the world probably never thinks
of her at all.
She wrote once,
that there are only two ideas
of order: the notion of what order is,
and, the attempt to conceptualize order,

but if you try to define the undefinable,
it becomes lost or removed from you.

Does anything have to do with anything?"

And the darkness . . .
the darkness continues.

Darkness

A book of poetry writing itself in the dark,
naming itself for the first time.
One word unable to read the next,
unable to read the rest, unable to finish the last.
A blind hand cradling a blind hand in the dark;
a blind hand writing a blind poem
for a hundred people lying in the dark,
unable to read the lines of their own covers.
A hundred nameless, noiseless covers, covering
cowards and cow manure waiting indeterminably
in the misty night for the misty morning,
when the sandy pearl moon,
lapped over by sandy waves of clouds
will eventually be swallowed by the oyster of dawn.
A hundred drunken wasteful spirits
eaten by uncleanly sheets and covers
infatuated with darkness.
A hundred sloppy, disappearing words,
blind of their compatriots, stagger
into their uninformed, uniformed, unfurling lines,
and covered by darkness.
A hundred bloodily deceased and decapitated soldiers
dialing home without fingers to their Viet Nam brothers,
lying in the dark for thirty years in dusty covers
in the dark, where seasons never skip
across furniture, never changing their dislike
for the light of the outdoors.
A hundred dispersed, unemptied trash cans
conversing, cursing obscenities in the dark absence
of emptied urban streets.
A hundred bent necks, a hundred burnt streets
a hundred collapsing forts, a hundred collapsing lies,
a hundred lonely awkward saviors and stone polishers
philosophizing scrawling awkward dialects of
words writing themselves in the dark.

81

A hundred leaning chairs, leaning on the darkness,
searching for a comfortable seat in the darkness,
on the darkness, and for the darkness.
A hundred lost companions, unspeakable,
unreadably lost, starving, tired, and misspelled
in the darkness of night,
not about to find their way.
A hundred nightly nights reminding each other
of a hundred satin shrugs forgetting the dusty dawn.
A hundred lonely maidens absent of light,
lost in darkness, absent of covers, lost in cold,
absent of all but the dark, wallowing wistfully
in the dark pages of small words
never able to find thoughts,
due to the eminent darkness;
never releasing cramped hands
or unused notebooks, unwriting themselves
empty into the darkness.
A hundred blind pens penning pennies
purposefully, cracking the crude crust of dawn.
A hundred dead Dillingers deserving death in the dark,
daily devouring descent dollars after dusk.
A hundred dolls easily evicted from their enormous
dollhouses, and having a silent teaparty in the dark.
Walt Whitman, orbiting satellites of statues
of wild savages in the dark of the river bank
of the minds of a hundred deceased soldiers,
deteriorating in their disillusioned darkness.
Dank, dirty dens dirtied by the dank dark of dawn.
A hundred missing mice mired in musty, mussy moss
lost in the darkness of dark, not about to find their way.
A hundred pilots absent of respectability,
desperate for swooping death in the darkness.
Darkness misspelling itself in the dark,
darkness expelling itself in the dark,
darkness repelling itself in the dark,
darkness fully revealing itself in the dark,
darkness stretched out nakedly,

under the covers of darkness.
A hundred rooms filled with womanudity
and vagrant husbands in the darkness
of urban streets, dressed in darkness.
There is always nothing left to write.
Nothing is ever light
and everything is always filled empty with plight,
hungry and sorry in the night.
A hundred candles void of light,
a hundred unrolled cigarettes
fearing the light,
unsure of what is right,
never wanting to be bright.
Oysterly dawns dawning
with sands and sounds.
A hundred unwritten, unshaven ravens
writing angry manifestos
to foreign worms, in the dark.
Dark aching alleys lit darkly, dingily, and dangerously
with alcohol crawling after bugs,
searching for a bed or a cover lover,
in the darkness, for the night.
No plight, no light, and a carcass full of fright,
and all chanting psalms, in the darkness
of palms under the shade of the tree of darkness.
A hundred cards playing tables in
endless darkness; darkness covered by darkness;
angels piercing darkness with darkness;
darkness chasing darkness with darkness;
darkness changing itself into darkness in the darkness,
and the dark shark of night,
swimming in darkness.
Buddha crying his hands into his head in darkness.
Vishnu crying his many many hands
into the Eye of Shiva in the dark.
Darkness spoiled by darkness;
a hundred spoiled candles, unlit and fading
into darkness, drowning in pumpkin salt and darkness.

The silent electric whir of darkness
weaving darkness into the dark.
A hundred thousand particles of unimaginable sensation
of undescribable magnitude wriggling through bodies,
starved for attention, lying dormant in the darkness.
Darkness, shrouded in darkness, swallowing sharks of darkness,
swimming in the shallow darkness.
Darkness lounging in the dark; too dark to sleep.
Darkness writing on itself in the darkness; too dark to see.
Darkness righting itself in the darkness.
Darkness lighting itself in darkness.
Darkness hungover from darkness.
Darkness appreciated only by darkness.
Darkness cooking in the stew of darkness,
basting itself, seasoning itself, savoring
and tasting itself for the first time.
Darkness finally coughing itself to sleep
in the abyss of darkness.

About the Author

Daniel Lutz was born in Libertyville, Illinois and is presently an English Major at the University of Iowa, in Iowa City, where he plans to attend the Writer's Workshop after graduation.

He has been writing since junior high school and hopes to continue publishing as a life long career.

Teach
me the words
and I'll sing
you the song.
Show
me the steps
and I'll perform
you the dance.
Offer me your friendship
and I'll always be loyal.
Grant me your love
and I will never leave.
Allow me to love you
and we can live a life
without doubt, without fear
and then we can share
what we've made with the world,
for blessed art thou and blessed am I.
Blessed are we and
blessed are all those who love
with the sounding of their hearts.

Angel of Harmony, Angel of Peace,
Angel of Discovery, lead us
to ourselves and help us to see
there is no life
without love.